AFRICA - BOTSWANA

CHOBE NATIONAL PARK

WWW.JEROME-HILLAIRE.COM
AF-BO-0006-EN

Caution

The writings in this «road book» are based on the experience of the author, Jerome Hillaire.

He can in no way be held responsible for the moral, physical or material damage that would occur to anyone reading this «road book».

- The information in this «road book» is true, but may change with time.

Copyright and trademark

The contents of this document cannot be copied, distributed or broadcasted, totally or partially, without the prior consent of the authors Eric CASTERA / Jérôme HILLAIRE.

The entire www.jerome-hillaire.com website and all the elements with the brand are protected by the trademark and copyright laws - INPI 4182593 registred 2015 ® JEROME HILLAIRE   CASTERA / HILLAIRE ©.

Introduction and ethics

**My name is Jerome Hillaire,
I am a professional guide, a naturalist, but above all a globetrotter.**

For over fifteen years, my passion for nature has led me to explore the most remote corners of the planet. During my travels, whether for work or pleasure, I often met tourists looking for information. They did not know how to get to some magical places, where you can observe legendary animals like lions or leopards. They did not know how to get ready to stay in remote areas.

That is why I want to share my experience. It is the result of a long process and you will not find it anywhere else. In these booklets, I have selected the most beautiful and the richest natural wildlife areas you can see on earth. If you follow my instructions, you will greatly increase your chances of flushing rare animals and you will discover magnificent landscapes for your great delight. Just like the Japanese tourist to whom I revealed where he would certainly see the last black rhinos in the African desert. This man told me he absolutely wanted to photograph this endangered species to show it to his grandchildren. He hoped that when they were adults, there would always be black rhinos in Africa.

Here you will find essential information **(simplified maps, the valuable GPS coordinates of the most remarkable sites in terms of wildlife and landscapes, essential tips about preparation and safety...)** in order to organize your adventure, and above all, to make it a truly memorable experience.

You will have the privilege to discover territories that are still wild and the animals that live there. I deeply hope that you will share my enthusiasm and my emotions. And you too will be convinced of the importance of preserving these special places, while nowadays our natural environment is increasingly threatened.

Dear globetrotters, I wish you a good trip !

Identity record

« CHOBE NATIONAL PARK »

CONTINENT : **AFRICA**
COUNTRY : **BOTSWANA**

Administrative capital : **GABORONE**
Official language : **ENGLISH**
Currency : **PULA**

REF : AF-BO-0006-EN

Discover the highest density of elephants in the world.

■ **GEOGRAPHIC FEATURES:**
The area of Chobe National Park is 11,700 km² (approximately 4,520 mi2).

■ **CLIMATE:**
The climate is tropical and arid with two well marked dry and wet seasons. Dry season from April to October. Wet season from November to March.

■ **TYPES OF LANDSCAPES :**
Dry shrub savannah, dry grassland, marshy areas, rivers, rocky chaos.

■ **SPECIES TO WATCH :**
Elephants, hippos, lions, leopards, cheetahs, wild dogs, servals, zebras, giraffes, impalas, buffaloes egrets, herons, geese, ducks, spoonbills, storks, kingfishers, crocodiles, bee-eaters, fish-eagles, etc.

Maps

IMPORTANT ! - **GPS COORDINATES** :

All the GPS coordinates listed in this booklet are represented by tiny red letters (**a,b,c,** etc.). You will find these letters on all the maps.

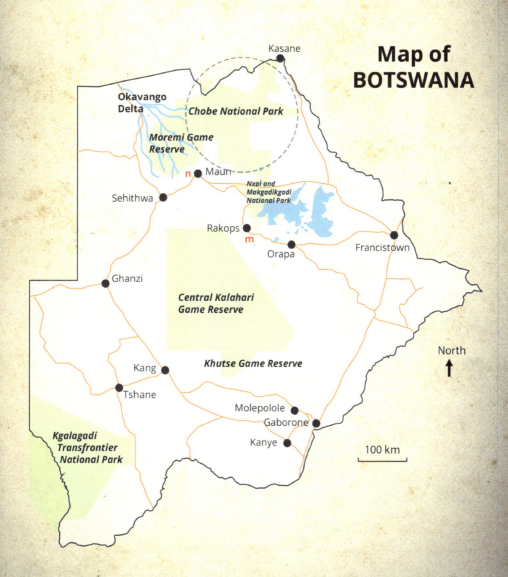

Discover the best animal observation areas and the finest sceneries
(green patterns on maps)

- Chobe River Front (nord Chobe)
- Savuti area (south Chobe)
- Boat ride on the river Chobe (north Chobe)

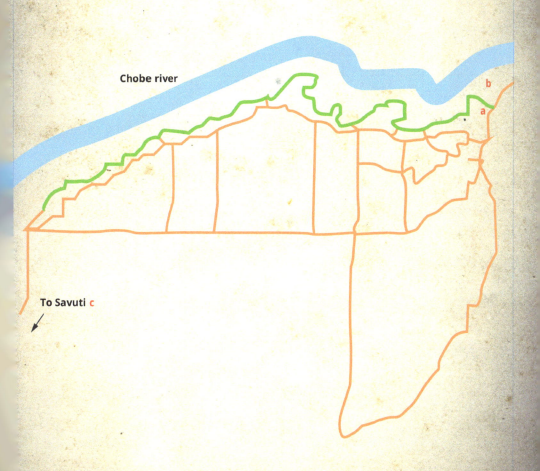

Chobe River Front

JH

EXCELLENT SPOT !

RECOMMENDED DURATION :
2 to 3 days.

GPS COORDONATES :
Chobe park entrance from the nearby town of Kasane
(a) 17° 50.601' S   25° 8.606'E

 DESCRIPTION OF THE LANDSCAPE :
A trail runs along the Chobe River. A succession of forests and grassy plains stretches along the river.

 ANIMALS YOU WILL WATCH :
You will be able to observe elephants, hippos, lions, zebras, giraffes, impalas, egrets, herons, geese, ducks, kingfishers, crocodiles, bee-eaters, fish-eagles, buffaloes, leopards, spoonbills, storks, etc.

Savuti aera

JH

XCELLENT SPOT !

RECOMMENDED DURATION :
2 to 3 days.

GPS COORDONATES :
(c) 18° 34.015' S   24° 3.901' E

DESCRIPTION OF THE LANDSCAPE :
South of the camping area, the trail which goes along the branch of the river and the swamps undoubtedly offers the most beautiful observations. All around, there are forests, savannah and bushes.

ANIMALS YOU WILL WATCH :
Savuti is one of the best places in Africa to see predators and the fauna of the savannah in general.

Boat ride on the Chobe River

EXCELLENT SPOT !

 RECOMMENDED DURATION :
1 day.

 GPS COORDONATES :
Ask someone at the reception desk of your campsite to organize this day out for you. In the town of Kasane, they all do.

 DESCRIPTION OF THE LANDSCAPE :
Tropical river on which focuses abundant and varied wildlife.

 ANIMALS YOU WILL WATCH :
Hippos, elephants, buffaloes, antelopes, many species of wetland birds, etc.

Informations

MAIN ENTRANCE :

Only a few kilometers from the town of Kasane :
(a) 17° 50.601'S   25° 8.606'E

ACCOMMODATION AND FACILITIES :

Several campsites and lodges are located in the town of Kasane just before the main entrance of the park. They all have running water, toilets and electricity.

Thebe campsite : **(b) 17° 47.176'S   25° 10.871'E**

Two bush campsites, named Ihaha and Savuti are located inside the park. Savuti is equipped with toilets and running water but there is no electricity. This campsite has a small shop where you can buy some food.

GENERAL RECOMMENDATIONS :

In the park (at Ihaha and Savuti), never leave your waste, your food or your kitchen utensils out of the vehicle, especially if you are absent. Some animals like jackals and hyenas might come and take it.

It can be very cold at night between May and October (-10 °), so take warm clothes.

In the park, remember that you are allowed to get out of your vehicle only in camping areas or in areas named «stretching point». However, always be careful not to get too far away from your vehicle or your tent because camping areas and «stretching points» are not fenced. Carnivores, elephants, hippos and buffaloes regularly go through these areas.

When you go out of your tent early in the morning, always check that there are no dangerous animals around, even if you are only going to the bathroom or to your car.

Informations

JH

RECOMMENDATIONS ON NAVIGATION :

It is not always easy to find your way there and the area near Savuti is very isolated.
Do not hesitate to get maps in different scales. For example, a general map of the country and another, more precise, to explore the selected area. Some maps must be purchased while others are sometimes included in the entrance of a national park, a tourist area or in an information center. In any case, remember that a map is always a good investment. It is a tool that I personally need, along with GPS.

About GPS, I personally advise to download the Tracks4Africa application, available on **http://tracks4africa.co.za.** This application makes it possible for you to view all your GPS tracks and roads of Africa and many other pieces of information (cities, accommodations, shops, banks, tricky sandy, muddy or rocky areas, etc.). This application is very detailed, but it is not free.

Another application a little less detailed, but free, is called «openstreetmap.»

http://www.openstreetmap.fr/   in french.

http://www.openstreetmap.org/   in English.

The other advantage of this app is that it covers the whole earth!

If you have a Garmin brand GPS, you can download and save to your GPS the countries that you need or worldwide on http://garmin.openstreetmap.nl/

Please note that on most tracks, it is difficult to drive over 30 kph. The distances being important, remember that it can take a long time to cover a relatively short mileage.

The track is very sandy in some places, especially in the north and in the south of Savuti. It is then easy to get stuck in the sand. Reduce tire pressure to 1 kg / cm2 and position your transmission on short gears («low range»). Thus, you should not have any problems.

The track is sometimes muddy near water streams. In Savuti, some streams can be crossed while some areas are not recommended because they are deep and very muddy. It is better to stay on the sandy tracks, which are numerous enough.

If you drive early in the morning, you will be less likely to get stuck in the sand. Indeed, because of the cool temperatures, the sand is much more compact.

Be careful you have enough petrol in your tank. Indeed, when you leave Kasane, you will no find any gas station until the town of Maun, much further south. For information, my vehicle fully loaded, used up to 20 liters / 100 km! Please calculate the proper amount according to the duration of the stay and the number of kilometers you think you will drive. Plan to take more petrol than necessary.

Informations

BEST TIME TO VISIT :

During the wet season, some tracks are impassable. It is impossible to go there, except possibly near the town of Kasane in an area called Chobe River Front.

During the dry season, many animals are concentrated around water sources for drinking.

You will be allowed to drive only from sunrise until sunset.

The dawn and late afternoons are unquestionably the two best times to see wildlife. During the hot hours of the day, most of the animals are in a period of reduced activity.

FINAL STOP :

In the north, you will get everything you need in the town of Kasane, as well as in the town of Maun in the south.

Informations

RESERVATIONS :

Try to book the Ihaha campsite (north of Chobe) and the Savuti campsite (south of Chobe) in advance, especially for the months of June, July, August and September.

For a daily visit to the park, you do not need to book one of the campsites in the town of Kasane. There is always room available throughout the year.

For the boat ride on the Chobe River, which I highly recommend, any of your campsites can organize it on request.

To book the Ihaha and Savuti campsites, check with :

For Ihaha contact
Tel/fax (00267) 6861448
E-mail: kwalatesafari@gmail.com

For savuti contact
Contact: (00267) 6865365
Fax: (00267) 686 5367
E-mail: reservations@sklcamps.co.bw gold sklcamps@botsnet.bw

Then email the invoice to D.W.N.P. in order to pay your entry fees.

Contact :

Departement of Wildlife and National Parks (D.W.N.P.) Parks and Reserves
Reservations Office P O Box 20364, Boseja, Maun, Botswana
Telephone No: (267) 6861265, Fax No.: (267) 6861264, Email: dwnp@gov.bw

Or :

Departement of Wildlife and National Parks (D.W.N.P.)
Parks and Reserves Reservations Office
P O Box 131, Gaborone, Botswana
Telephone No: (267) 3180774, Fax No: (267) 3180775, Email: dwnp@gov.bw

However all entrance fees in parks must be paid to the D.W.N.P.

Since changes are always possible in the camping agencies, the best thing to do is to contact the D.W.N.P first so that they can explain the procedure.

Highlights

HIGHLIGHTS DURING MY VISIT TO THE RESERVE :

The observation of the highest density of elephants in the world.

On the riverbank, a pack of ten lions devouring an elephant in front of two hippos that kept growling.

The same pack of lions chasing away a spotted hyena which was trying to steal a piece of meat.

The unsuccessful hunt for a leopard which had approached a group of impalas.

A couple raptors harassing a group of guineafowls.

The countless wetland birds omnipresent on wetlands.

The couple of Klipspringer antelopes that moved discreetly on rocks.

The boat ride on the Chobe River from the town of Kasane makes it possible to discover an exceptionally rich fauna.

Highlights

 HIGHLIGHTS DURING MY VISIT TO THE RESERVE :

The boat ride on the Chobe River never disappoints.

Highlights

HIGHLIGHTS DURING MY VISIT TO THE RESERVE :

The fish-eagles are present all along the river. You will often hear their shrill call.

Highlights

JH

 HIGHLIGHTS DURING MY VISIT TO THE RESERVE :

On the bank, look for crocodiles. Large specimens are often visible.

Highlights

 HIGHLIGHTS DURING MY VISIT TO THE RESERVE :

Many predators follow the herds of herbivores.

Highlights

 HIGHLIGHTS DURING MY VISIT TO THE RESERVE :

Chobe Park is home to the largest population of elephants in the world.

Highlights

 HIGHLIGHTS DURING MY VISIT TO THE RESERVE :

Very cute dwarf mongooses ran away for a hiding place when I arrived.

Highlights

JH

HIGHLIGHTS DURING MY VISIT TO THE RESERVE :

I very much like to hear the song of this lark! I have heard it so often in wildlife documentaries. This time, I can listen to it for real.

Highlights

 HIGHLIGHTS DURING MY VISIT TO THE RESERVE :

The many lions in Chobe are often to be heard and seen.

FIND THE OTHER AVAILABLE BOOKLETS
on the website : www.jerome-hillaire.com

The most beautiful wilderness areas
Iceland, Costa Rica, Namibia
USA, Canary islands, etc.

Specialized books like «A Guide for Safe Travelling», «Recommendations for the Exploration of the African Bush by Car», which explain how to protect yourself from all the dangers you may face while travelling (safety, health, swindles, breakdowns, adequate attitude with the police, etc.)

You can also find all the books and movies by the author including :

«9 mois en Amazonie »   French version   « 9 months in the Amazon, the photo album»
«1 an dans le bush africain » French version   «1 Year in the Heart of the African Bush, the photo

« Mission Tambopata, which destiny for the macaws ? » Documentary 52'
« Candamo, in the footsteps of the Amazonian fauna » Documentary 52'

ALL OUR PARTNERS will offer preferential rates (travel deals, equipment, car rental etc.)
on **www.jerome-hillaire.com**

Production : Eric CASTERA, Jérôme HILLAIRE
Author : Jérôme HILLAIRE, Karelle THOMAS
Credits : Jérôme HILLAIRE
Sales and advertising department : VISIO40 Service
Art direction : Eric CASTERA
Design : OTIDEA Service
Executive office : VISIO40 Service

Copyright © JUNE 2015 CASTERA / HILLAIRE - All rights reserved.

The contents of this document cannot be copied, distributed or broadcasted, totally or partially, without the prior consent of the authors Eric CASTERA / Jérôme HILLAIRE.

The entire www.jerome-hillaire.com website and all the elements with the brand are protected by the trademark and copyright laws - INPI 4182593 registred 2015 ® JEROME HILLAIRE   CASTERA / HILLAIRE ©.

Printed in the USA
CPSIA information can be obtained
at www.ICGtesting.com
LVHW070302301023
762436LV00027B/13